NOVENA

Saint Alphonsus Liguori

A REDEMPTORIST PASTORAL PUBLICATION
ADAPTED BY DAVID WERTHMANN

ONE LIGUORI DRIVE
LIGUORI MO 63057-9999

Imprimi Potest:
Richard Thibodeau, C.Ss.R.
Provincial, Denver Province
The Redemptorists

ISBN 0-7648-1095-2
© 2003, Liguori Publications
Printed in the United States of America
03 04 05 06 07   5 4 3 2 1

All rights reserved. No part of this pamphlet may be reproduced, stored in a retrieval system, or transmitted without the written permission of Liguori Publications.

Scripture quotations are from the *New Revised Standard Version of the Bible*, © 1989 by the Division of Christian Education of the National Council of Churches of Christ in the USA. Used with permission. All rights reserved.

To order, call 1-800-325-9521
www.liguori.org
www.catholicbooksonline.com

Introduction

Saint Alphonsus Liguori wrote a number of novenas for use during the seasons of Advent and Christmas. His intention was that we should use the meditations written for each day of the novena as a form of spiritual reading or as quiet periods of meditative prayer to prepare our hearts for the coming of Christ on Christmas. The goal is to guide us in using our religious imaginations so that we may have a meaningful and deeply personal appreciation of the mystery of the Incarnation.

This novena is meant to engage the whole person: physically, emotionally, intellectually, spiritually, and socially. Reciting the chaplet vocally at the beginning of each session can bring the corporal dimension of our lives into our prayer. The daily meditations engage our imagination and reasoning powers. The Affections and Prayers address our emotions. It is generally intended that a novena session should take place against a backdrop of silence so that our hearts can listen to the Holy Spirit's voice in the empty spaces beneath the words of the meditation. Finally, praying the novena with a group calls in the social dimension of our lives.

How to Use This Novena

∽

The novena is meant to go from December 16-24, the nine days before Christmas, and can be done either privately or as a group. The general tone for the novena is set by a short chaplet to be recited at the beginning of each day's session. This string of prayers consists of nine brief invocations to Jesus, describing him under some aspect of the mystery of the Incarnation, and followed by the response: "Have mercy on us." Each response is then followed by a vocal or silent recitation of the well-known Catholic prayers: the "Our Father," a "Hail Mary," and a "Glory Be." This repetition of prayers helps to prevent the mind from wandering and prepares the heart for what is to come. The general purpose of the chaplet is to create an atmosphere of prayer so that the various meditations can unfold.

The meditation for each day concentrates on some particular aspect of the Incarnation and is followed by a series of fervent expressions of love and devotion called "Affections and Prayers." There are no other closing prayers, because in that way the novena is open-ended and flows right into the celebration of Christmas itself. Since each day of the novena focuses on a different aspect of the mystery of the Incarnation, one can say that through this little devotion, our celebration of Christmas has already begun.

Chaplet to be recited before every meditation

Leader: O Jesus, who was born in a cave and laid upon straw in a manger, have mercy on us.

Response: Have mercy on us.

Our Father…; Hail Mary…; Glory be…
Leader: O Jesus, who was presented and offered by Mary in the Temple, and who was also sacrificed for us on the cross, have mercy on us.
Response: Have mercy on us.

Our Father…; Hail Mary…; Glory be…
Leader: O Jesus, who was persecuted by Herod and forced to flee into Egypt, have mercy on us.
Response: Have mercy on us.

Our Father…; Hail Mary…; Glory be…
Leader: O Jesus, who lived in Egypt for seven years, poor, unknown, and despised, have mercy on us.
Response: Have mercy on us.

Our Father…; Hail Mary…; Glory be…
Leader: O Jesus, who returned to your own country to one day be crucified between two thieves, have mercy on us.
Response: Have mercy on us.

Our Father…; Hail Mary…; Glory be…
Leader: O Jesus, who at age twelve remained in

the Temple to debate with the doctors, and after three days was found by your mother, Mary, have mercy on us.

Response: Have mercy on us.

Our Father…; Hail Mary…; Glory be…
Leader: O Jesus, who lived hidden from the world for so many years in the workshop at Nazareth, serving Mary and Joseph, have mercy on us.

Response: Have mercy on us.

Our Father…; Hail Mary…; Glory be…
Leader: O Jesus, who went about preaching and teaching the way of salvation for three years before your passion and death, have mercy on us.

Response: Have mercy on us.

Our Father…; Hail Mary…; Glory be…
Leader: O Jesus, who died on a cross for love of us, have mercy on us.

Response: Have mercy on us.

Our Father… Hail Mary…; Glory be…

Meditation One

December 16

The love that God has shown to us in becoming human.

Think about the great love God has shown us by becoming human in order to obtain eternal life for us.

Our first parents, Adam and Eve, rebelled against God and were driven out of paradise. As a result, they and all of us, their descendants, were condemned to everlasting death. But the Son of God, grieving because humanity was lost, took upon himself our human flesh. Then, in order to save us from death, he died on a cross, condemned as a criminal.

We might imagine God the Father saying to his Son, "My child, consider the hardships you will have to undergo while on earth. You will be born in a cold cave, with no place to be laid except in the trough where animals come to feed. As an infant, you will have to flee to Egypt to escape the hands of Herod. After returning, you will have to live in a workshop as a poor, humble servant. And finally, worn out by sufferings, you will have to give up your life, dying on a cross, insulted and forsaken by all."

And Jesus would respond, "Father, it does not matter. I am happy to endure whatever comes, provided that humanity is saved."

How would we react if a millionaire took compassion on a dead worm and chose to become a worm himself, offering his own blood as a transfusion, and died in order to restore life to the other worm? Yet the eternal Word has done even more than that for us. God, the Creator, has become like us, one of his own creatures, to share in our human life, so that we can share once again in his divine life. When God realized that all the natural gifts he had bestowed on us could not win our love for him, he became one of us and gave himself entirely to us. *The Word became flesh, and lived among us* (John 1:14a).

Through sin, humanity separated itself from God. But God, because of his great love for us, came from heaven to seek us. Why? In order that we might realize how much God loves us, and in gratitude love God in return. Any time a cat or a dog comes to us from across the room, we can't help but respond by petting it and speaking to it. So why do we ignore God, who comes to us all the way from heaven?

Once, when a priest proclaimed the words, "and the Word became flesh," someone in the church neglected to make a proper reverence. This prompted the devil to give that person a blow, saying, "Oh, ungrateful one! If only God had done for me what he has done for you, I would remain with my head always bowed down in thanksgiving."

Affections and Prayers

Son of God, you became human in order to make yourself lovable to us. But where is the love that we should have for you in return? After all, you have given your life to save us. Yet, why are we so indifferent to your presence? I admit that I myself have not always paid attention to you, your love, or your gifts. But your birth, your death and Resurrection, the gift of Eucharist, provide me with hope. Forgive the times that I have failed to acknowledge your influence in my life.

I love you, O Incarnate Word. I love you, O my

God. I love you, O Infinite Goodness. And I ask forgiveness for all the sins that I have committed, large and small, public or private. I wish that I could die for you.

Dear Jesus, give me the gift of love for you. Let me never again feel complacent over the trials you endured for me. I want to love you always. Give me perseverance in loving you.

O Mary, Mother of God and my mother too, obtain for me from your son the grace to love him always, even unto death.

Meditation Two

DECEMBER 17

The love of God in being born as an infant.

The Son of God, in becoming human for our sake, might have appeared in the world at the age of a grown man, the way Adam appeared when he was created. But since children usually attract greater love to themselves from those who take care of them, Jesus chose to appear on earth as an infant; and as the poorest and most miserable infant ever born. Saint Peter Chrysologous wrote: "Our God chose to be born this way because he wanted to be loved." The prophet Isaiah had already predicted that the Son of God was to be born an infant and give himself entirely to us through the love he bore for us: *A child is born to us, a son is given to us* (Isaiah 9:6a).

O my Jesus, almighty and true God, what else could possibly have attracted you to come from heaven and be born in a cave, if not your love for us? What convinced you to leave the lap of your Father and lay yourself down in a manger? What drew you down from your throne above the stars to stretch yourself out on a little pile of straw? What, from the midst of the nine choirs of angels, has placed you between these sheep and oxen? You inflame the seraphim with holy fire, yet look, you tremble from the cold in this stable! You give the sun, the stars, and the planets their paths of movement, yet now you cannot move at all without being carried in someone's arms! You provide food for all creatures, and yet now you depend on a little milk to sustain your life. You are the delight of heaven, and yet how is it that I now hear you whimper and cry? Tell me, who has reduced you to such lowliness? "Who has done this? Love has done it," says Saint Bernard. Yes, the love that you have for us has done it.

Affections and Prayers

O dearest Infant, tell me what you came on earth to do. Tell me whom you are seeking. Ah, yes, I now understand…you have come to die for me, a lost sheep, in order that I may no more hide from you, but love you. O Jesus, my treasure, my life, my love, my all, if I do not love you, then whom shall I love? Where can I find a mother or father, a friend, or a spouse more loving than you? And who has ever loved me more than you have? I am sorry that I have lived so many years in this world and yet still love you so little, even having offended you and sometimes forgotten you. Forgive me, O my beloved Redeemer, for I regret that I have ever treated you so badly. I am sorry with all my heart. Forgive me, and give me your grace so that I may never again separate myself from you, and so that I may love you constantly for the rest of my life. O my love, I give myself to you entirely. Accept me, Lord, and do not reject me, even though I might deserve it.

O Mary, you are my advocate. You always obtain whatever you ask from your son. Beg him to forgive me, and to help me persevere until death.

Meditation Three

∞

DECEMBER 18

The life of poverty which Jesus lived, even from his birth.

God planned that when his Son was to be born on earth an edict would be promulgated by the emperor, obliging the head of every household to go to the place of his birth and register. And so, Joseph had to go with his wife to Bethlehem, to enroll according to the decree of Caesar. While there, Mary's time of delivery arrived. Because she had been driven from all the other houses and even from the common shelter for poor people, she ended up spending the night in a cave, and there gave birth to the King of Heaven.

It is true that Jesus would have been just as poor if he had been born in Nazareth. But at least there he would have had a dry room, a little fire, warm clothes, and a comfortable cradle. But no, he chose to be born in a cold cavern without a fire to warm him. He chose to have the livestock's manger for his cradle, and a little prickly straw for his bedding, in order that he might experience what poor people have to experience.

Let us enter that cave in Bethlehem, but let us enter with faith. If we go without faith we will see nothing but a poor infant, who moves us to compassion by seeing him so beautiful, but shivering with cold and crying from the itchiness of the straw on which he lies. But if we enter with faith, we will believe that this child is the Son of God, who loved us so much that he came down to earth and endured so much to pay for our sins. How could we not thank him and love him?

Affections and Prayers

O sweet infant, how can I be so ungrateful to you and offend you so often, knowing how much you have done for me? But the tears you cried, and the poverty you chose to endure out of love for me, give me hope in the forgiveness of all the sins that I have committed. I regret, my Jesus, that I have turned my back on you and on my sisters and brothers so often. I love you above all other things. You are my God and my all! From this day forward, you will be my only treasure and my only good. With Saint Ignatius of Loyola, I will say, "Give me your love, give me your grace, and I will be rich." I wish for and I desire nothing else. You alone are sufficient for me, my Jesus, my life, my love.

O Mary, so close to Jesus, help me to be greatful for the gift of faith in your son.

Meditation Four

DECEMBER 19

The life of humility which Jesus lived, even from his infancy.

All the clues that the angels gave the shepherds to help them find the Savior, who had just been born, were marks of humility: *This will be a sign for you: you will find a child wrapped in bands of cloth and lying in a manger* (Luke 2:12). This is how you will find the newborn Messiah, the angel said. You will find him as an infant, wrapped in poor ragged clothes, in a stable, lying on straw in a manger for animals. That is how the King of Heaven, the Son of God, was born, because he came to destroy the pride that had been the cause of humanity's spiritual ruin.

The prophets foretold that our Redeemer would be treated as the most wretched person on earth, and that he would be overwhelmed with insults. How much ridicule Jesus had to tolerate because of us! He was treated as a drunkard, as a magician, as a blasphemer, and a heretic. Think of how many insults he had to endure during his passion. He was abandoned by his own disciples. One of them even sold him for thirty pieces of silver, and another denied having ever known him. He was led through the streets bound like a criminal, scourged like a slave, treated like a madman, and mocked as a bogus king. He was struck, spit upon in the face, and finally he was put to death on a cross, suspended between two thieves. One would think that he had been the greatest lawbreaker the world had ever seen.

Saint Bernard commented that the noblest of all men, Jesus Christ, was treated like the most depraved person of all. "But, my Jesus," he adds, "the more degraded you are, the more dear you are to me." The more humbled and despised he appears, the more esteemed and worthy of our love he becomes.

Affections and Prayers

O sweet Savior, you have embraced so much disgrace for love of me, and yet I cannot bear a word of insult without immediately thinking of revenge—I, who often deserve to be trampled underfoot by all those whom I have harmed. I am ashamed of appearing before you, such an arrogant sinner that I am. O Lord, do not drive me from your presence, as I deserve. You have promised that you cannot condemn a heart that repents and humbles itself. I regret all the offences I have ever committed against you or against my neighbor. Forgive me, Jesus, for I will not offend you or anyone else ever again. You have put up with so many wounds for my sake. For your sake, I will bear all the difficulties that may come my way.

I love you, my Jesus; you who endured such evil for my sake. I love you, my Good, above every other good. Give me your help, that I may always love you and that I may endure every trial for love of you.

O Mary, recommend me to your son. Pray to Jesus for me.

Meditation Five

∞

DECEMBER 20

The life of sorrow which Jesus lived, even from his birth.

Jesus could have saved us without suffering and without dying. But he willingly chose a life full of tribulations to show how much he loved us. The prophet Isaiah called him the man of sorrows (Isaiah 53:3) because the life of Christ was to be full of woe. His passion did not begin at the time of his death, but from the beginning of his life.

Imagine Jesus, as soon as he was born, lying in a stable, where everything caused distress for him. His sight was troubled because he could see nothing in that cave but dark, rough walls. His sense of smell was haunted by the stench of dung from the animals lying nearby. His skin was irritated by the itchy straw that served as his bed. Soon after birth, he was forced to flee to Egypt, where he lived several years of his childhood, poor, and despised as a foreigner. The life he led afterward in Nazareth was not much better. Then consider how his life ended in Jerusalem, dying in anguish on a cross.

So the life of Jesus was one of continual anxiety—even worse than that, because he had constantly before his eyes all the sadness that would be his on the day of his death. One day a nun, complaining before the crucifix, said to him, "O Lord, you remained on the cross for three hours, but I have suffered my pain for several years." Jesus answered her, "What you have said shows how unaware you are. I suffered even from my mother's womb all the pains of my life and death." But because Jesus voluntarily chose those afflictions, they did not hurt him as much as did the sight of our sins and our ingratitude for his great love. One particular saint could never stop lamenting over the offenses she committed against God. Her confessor said to her, "Cease crying. God has already forgiven you." But she replied, "How can I cease crying when I know that my sins kept Jesus in a state of agony all his life?"

Affections and Prayers

O my sweet Love, did my sins keep you in a state of agony during all of your earthly life? Then, tell me what I can do so that you will forgive me, for I will leave nothing undone. I regret all the offenses I have ever committed against you, O my greatest Good. I repent, and I love you more than I love myself. I feel a great desire to love you. You have given me this desire, so now give me the strength to love you even more intensely. It is only just that I, who have offended you so much, should also love you so much. Remind me constantly of the love you have for me, so that my soul may always burn with love for you, and so that I may think of you alone, desire you alone, and strive to please you alone.

O God of Love, I was once a slave to this world. But now I give myself entirely to you. Accept me in your mercy, and from this day forward bind me with your love, O Jesus. I will love you while I live, and in loving you, I will die.

O Mary, my mother and my hope, help me to love Jesus. This alone is the favor I desire and ask from you.

Meditation Six

DECEMBER 21

*The mercy of God in coming
from heaven to save us by his death.*

Saint Paul says *the goodness and loving kindness of God our Savior appeared* (Titus 3:4). It was then, when the Son of God made man appeared on earth, that we saw how great the goodness of God is toward us. Saint Bernard wrote that the power of God first appeared through the creation of the world, and sustaining the world has shown God's wisdom. But God's mercy appeared to an even greater degree when God took human flesh to save lost humanity by his sufferings and death. And what greater mercy could the Son of God have shown us than to take upon himself the pains we have deserved?

Imagine him as a newborn infant, wrapped in swaddling clothes in a manger, unable to move or feed himself. Just to survive, he relied on Mary to feed him with a little milk. Imagine him many years later, in the judgment hall before Pilate, bound to a column by ropes from which he could not loosen himself, and scourged from head to foot. Imagine him on the journey to Calvary, falling down as he went along the road, from weakness, and from the weight of the cross that he carried. Finally, imagine him nailed to that infamous tree upon which he finished his life, in agony and suffering.

Jesus Christ wished to gain all the endearments of our hearts by his love for us, and therefore he would not send an angel to redeem us, but came himself, to save us by his passion and Resurrection. If an angel had been our redeemer we would have a divided heart—loving God as our creator and the angel as our redeemer. But because God, who is our Creator, wants our whole heart, he chose to also be our Redeemer.

Affections and Prayers

O my Redeemer, where would I now be if you had not shown me so much patience, but instead had condemned me to death while I was still in sin? Since you have waited for me, O Jesus, forgive me now and quickly, before death surprises me while I am still guilty of so many offenses against you. I regret, O my greatest Good, having ignored your

Word and your commands. I feel like I could die of shame over my sins. But I also know that you cannot ever forsake anyone who seeks you. If I have failed you in any serious way in my life, I resolve from now on to seek only you, and to love only you.

Yes, dear God, I love you above all things. I love you more than I love myself. Help me, Lord, to love you always for the rest of my entire life. I ask for nothing more, and I trust that you will grant it.

Mary, my hope, please pray for me; for if you do, I am certain to receive God's grace.

Meditation Seven

DECEMBER 22

The journey of the Infant Jesus to Egypt.

The Son of God came from heaven to save humanity. But no sooner was he born, than they began to persecute him, even unto death.

Herod, afraid that this Infant would take away his kingdom, tried to put the child to death. So in a dream, an angel advised Saint Joseph to take Jesus and his mother to Egypt. Informing Mary, Joseph promptly obeyed. He took along with him the tools of his trade that he had available, to use in providing a livelihood for himself and his poor family while in Egypt. For her part, Mary packed a small bag of clothes for the holy Infant. Then, drawing near the crib with tears, she said to her sleeping child, "O my son and my God, you have come down from heaven to save humanity, yet hardly after you are born they already seek to take away your life."

That very night, still crying, she took the baby Jesus, and she and Joseph set off on their journey.

Think about how much these lonely pilgrims must have suffered while making such a long journey, deprived of every comfort. The infant was not yet able to walk, so Mary and Joseph had to take turns carrying him in their arms. During the journey through the desert of Egypt, their only bed at night was the bare earth in the open air. The Infant wept in the cold, and Joseph and Mary also wept out of compassion for him. Who would not weep, after all, seeing the Son of God, poor and persecuted, wandering about on the earth so that he would not be killed by his enemies?

Affections and Prayers

O dearest infant Jesus, I hear you cry. And you ought to cry, being neglected by your very own creatures whom you love so much!

O my God, I have also neglected you and sinned against you. But now I resolve to love you even more than I love myself. And there can be no sorrow greater than that which I suffer, recalling how I have ignored you, my greatest Good. Please forgive me, my Jesus, and allow me to carry you in my heart during the rest of my life's journey, so that I may enter eternity with you as an essential part of my life.

I have so often turned away from you through sin. From now on I will love you above all other things. I repent of all the ways I have ever ignored or offended you by hurting someone else.

My beloved Lord, I will never ignore you again. Give me strength to resist temptations. Do not allow me to turn from you. I would rather die than do something that offends you or my neighbor.

O Mary, my hope, help me to live always in response to God's love.

Meditation Eight

DECEMBER 23

*The sojourn of the Infant Jesus
in Egypt and Nazareth.*

Our blessed Redeemer spent his infancy in Egypt, living there for seven years in poverty and contempt. Joseph and Mary were unknown there, with neither relatives nor friends. And they could scarcely earn enough to get by through the labor of their hands. Their cottage was poor, their bed was poor, and their food was poor. In this humble hut, Mary weaned Jesus. At first she fed him from her breast. Later on, she took a little bread soaked in water and placed it in his mouth. It was in that cottage that she made his first little garment, taking off his swaddling clothes and dressing him in regular ones. In that cottage, the child Jesus took his first steps, although he kept faltering and toppling many times, just as other children do. There, also, he uttered his first words, but with hesitation.

Imagine what God has reduced himself to for

love of us! God, stumbling and falling as he walked! God, stammering while he spoke!

The life Jesus led at the house in Nazareth after his return from Egypt was much the same: poor and humiliating. Until age thirty, he was a simple shop boy, obeying Joseph and Mary. *And he was obedient to them* (Luke 2:51). Jesus went to fetch water; Jesus opened and closed the shop; Jesus swept the house; he gathered wood for the fire, and worked all day helping Joseph.

Imagine God living as a boy! God sweeping the floor! God sweating as he planed a piece of wood! And who was he? The all-powerful God, who with a simple nod created the whole universe, and who could destroy it just as easily if he wished! Should not the mere thought of this move our hearts to love him?

How inspiring it must have been to watch the devotion with which Jesus said his prayers, the patience with which he labored, the haste in which he obeyed, the moderation he used in eating, and the kindness and charity with which he spoke and interacted with others! Every word, every action of Jesus was so virtuous that it filled everyone around him with love for God—but especially Mary and Joseph, who were constantly with him!

Affections and Prayers

O Jesus, my Savior! I realize that you, who are my God, lived for many years unknown and looked down upon in poverty because of your love for me. How, then, can I desire the pleasures, honors, and riches of the world? Although they are not bad things, I renounce them all, and I want to be your companion here on earth—poor like you, humble like you, and despised like you. Then I hope to one day enjoy your company in heaven. After all, what can the kingdoms or the treasures of earth amount to? My Jesus, you will be my only treasure, my only Good.

I greatly regret the many times in the past that I have disregarded your friendship while satisfying my own desires. Now I repent with all my heart. From now on, I would be willing to die a thousand times over rather than destroy my relationship with you. My God, I want to offend you no more. I want to love you always. Help me be faithful to you for the rest of my life.

Sweet Mary! You are the refuge of sinners. You are my hope.

Meditation Nine

◯

DECEMBER 24

The birth of the Infant Jesus in the cave of Bethlehem.

Since the Roman emperor's edict said that everyone was to enroll in his own country, Joseph and his wife, Mary, departed for Bethlehem. The trip took four days, traveling over mountainous roads in the cold of winter wind and rain. Think of how much the Blessed Virgin must have suffered on that journey.

As soon as they arrived, the time of her delivery was at hand, so Joseph went around the town looking for lodging where Mary could give birth to her child. But, because they were poor, they were driven away by everyone, even from the inn where poor people were normally sheltered. So they left the town and found a cave. As Mary entered, Joseph protested, saying, "My dear wife, how can you spend the night in this cold, damp place? Can't you see that this is a stable for animals?" But she answered, "Joseph, this shed is the royal palace where the Son of God chooses to be born."

And since the time for the birth had arrived, the Holy Virgin was in prayer. Suddenly the cave became brilliantly lit, as if by the sun or a star, and the Son of God came forth into the world as a tender infant, crying and trembling with cold. The first thing Mary did was to adore him as her God. Then she held him to her bosom, and wrapped him in swaddling clothes that she had brought along. Finally, she laid him on a little straw in the manger.

That is how the Son of the eternal God chose to be born for love of us.

A saint once said that those who love Jesus Christ most ought to kneel at the feet of the Holy Child and, in spirit, perform for him the same service as the beasts in the stable at Bethlehem who warmed him with their breath. We should warm him with our sighs of love.

Affections and Prayers

O dearest infant Jesus, I hear you cry. And you ought to cry, being neglected by your very own creatures whom you love so much!

O my God, I have also neglected you and sinned

against you. But now I resolve to love you even more than I love myself. And there can be no sorrow greater than that which I suffer, recalling how I have ignored you, my greatest Good. Please forgive me, my Jesus, and allow me to carry you in my heart during the rest of my life's journey, so that I may enter eternity with you as an essential part of my life.

I have so often turned away from you through sin. From now on I will love you above all other things. I repent of all the ways I have ever ignored or offended you by hurting someone else.

My beloved Lord, I will never ignore you again. Give me strength to resist temptations. Do not allow me to turn from you. I would rather die than do something that offends you or my neighbor.

O Mary, my hope, help me to live always in response to God's love.